THE
GOOD
SAMARITAN

ARCH Books

© 1964 CONCORDIA PUBLISHING HOUSE, ST. LOUIS, MISSOURI

LIBRARY OF CONGRESS CATALOG CARD NO. 63-23369
MANUFACTURED IN THE UNITED STATES OF AMERICA
ALL RIGHTS RESERVED   ISBN 0-570-06000-1

THE GOOD SAMARITAN

Luke 10:25-37 FOR CHILDREN

Written by Janice Kramer

Illustrated by Sally Mathews

Over in the Holy Land,
so many years ago,
a merchant from Jerusalem
went down to Jericho.
He started out one lovely morn
as dawn began to break;
his little donkey carried
all the things he had to take.

The trip was rather pleasant
as they went down their way;
the merchant thought of all the things
that he would do that day.
He had some goods to trade and sell
and many things to buy;
he hoped to get to Jericho
before the night drew nigh.

But little did the merchant know
that farther down the road
a band of robbers eyed with greed
the little donkey's load.
Alert, with evil hearts, they watched
and waited till at last
the unsuspecting merchant and his beast
were walking past.

The leader of the bandits
gave a terrifying shout,
and with this sign the thugs emerged
and suddenly jumped out.

With great big clubs they beat the man;
they beat him till he bled,
then took his donkey, stole his goods,
and left him almost dead.

A silence settled over all,
the merchant was alone;
he lay there suffering by the road,
and no one heard him moan.
Too weak and dazed to help himself,
all he could do was wait;
would no one come along to help
before it was too late?

But down the road there came a man,
and he was drawing near;
at last the bleeding merchant thought
that help was really here!

It was a priest in purple robes,
hands folded as in prayer;
a priest would help the wounded man,
a priest would surely care!

His shuffling footsteps on the road
produced the only sound
while silent was the wounded man
so helpless on the ground.
The priest was busy praying,
his eyes were both shut tight.
But one eye chanced to open
and saw the sorry sight.

"Oh, what a shame!" the priest observed;
"I cannot stop today,
or I'll be late for service.
I must be on my way!
I'm sure that someone will come soon,
so I'll just let him lie."

And carefully
and quietly
he tiptoed right on by.

The merchant was alone again;
was this to be the end?
But then another man came down
the road and round the bend.
He was a Levite,* who helped the priests,
he sure would understand
that here and now he ought to stop
and lend a helping hand.

*A temple assistant

The Levite halted in his tracks,
his eyes grew very wide.
His heart was warm with pity
and felt a pain inside.
He stood there undecided;
he knew he ought to stay,
but what he really wanted was
to turn and run away.

"This truly is a horrid sight,"
the troubled Levite said.
"I really do believe he ought
to be at home in bed.
But I'm no doctor, mercy me,
I might do something wrong!
Besides,

I feel quite sick myself —
I'd better run along."

The day was drawing to an end,
and night was coming on;
the merchant now would surely die,
for every hope was gone.
But as the shadows of the night
displaced the light of day,
another man came down the road
by which the merchant lay.

This man was from Samaria,
his people long had been
despised and hated by the merchant
and all his countrymen.
The chance that this Samaritan
would help was very slim;
he surely wouldn't want to help
a man who hated him!

But as he came around the bend,
he stopped with great surprise;
for when he saw the merchant there,
he hardly could believe his eyes.
"How can it be? This wounded man
is out here all alone;
I would have come here sooner, friend,
if I had only known!"

And then the kind Samaritan
got down upon his knee;
he tried the very best he could
to help his enemy.

He gently bound each bloody wound
and tried to ease the pain;
oh, surely, it would be too bad
if he had helped in vain!

But when he'd given all the help
that he knew how to give,
he saw that now, without a doubt,
the wounded man would live!
He gently placed the merchant on
his donkey's back, and then
the two men and the donkey small
went down the road again.

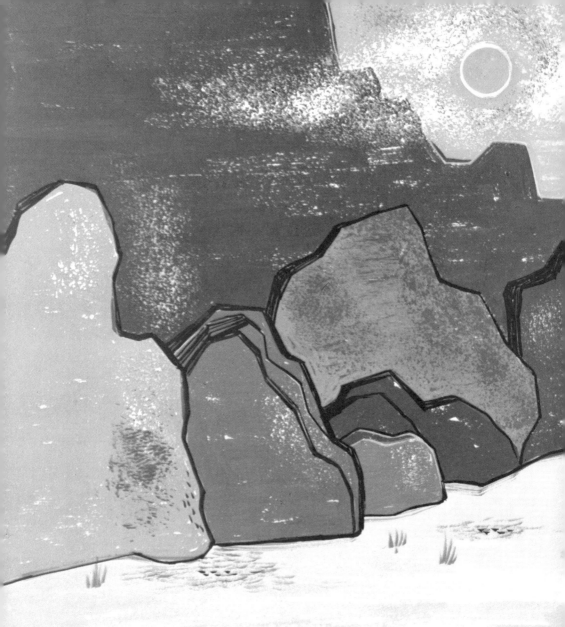

They had to travel very slow.
It was a lonely night.
At last this kind Samaritan
beheld a welcome sight.

He saw a warm and cozy inn
beside the road ahead;
he took the merchant to the inn
and put him right to bed.

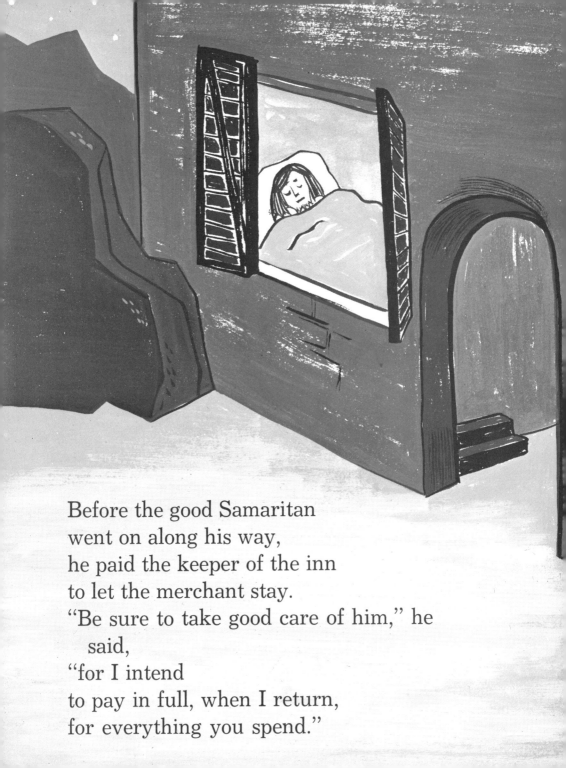

Before the good Samaritan
went on along his way,
he paid the keeper of the inn
to let the merchant stay.
"Be sure to take good care of him," he
    said,
"for I intend
to pay in full, when I return,
for everything you spend."

"Now," asked our Lord,
"*Who* helped his fellowman
in every way he could?
Who was the one who acted here
the way a *neighbor* should?"
The priest, you'll say, was not the one—
he hurried right on by;
nor did the Levite help the man—
he seemed afraid to try.

The good Samaritan—he was
the only one to stay;
and though the merchant hated him,
he helped him anyway.
How wonderful if you and I
and all God's children would
show such a love to all we meet
as Jesus said we should!

Dear Parents:

We are to love our neighbor, the Great Commandment tells us. What does this mean? Does this include people who are not one of us, those of another race and religion, those who look down on us or we on them?

Because people were confused about this, Jesus told our parable. The hero of the story is a member of a people despised and hated by Jesus' nation because the Samaritans' race and religion were not pure.

Can you help your child understand the lesson taught in this parable? Can you help him carry out the sometimes difficult task of being a true neighbor, as the Samaritan was, even to those who may not seem our brothers, our "neighbors"? You may want to read to your child, or help him read it himself, the story of the Good Samaritan in your Bible. (Luke 10:30-37)

THE EDITOR